I0479329

Table of Contents

Definition of Recycling

Recycling is the process of collecting and processing materials that would otherwise be thrown away as trash and turning them into new products. (US EPA, 2020)

Recycling not only benefits the environment but also have a positive effect on the economy. Recycling is reported throughout human history but has come a long way since the time of Plato when humans reused broken tools and pottery when materials were scarce.

Wikipedia defines Recycling as,

"Recycling is the process of converting waste materials into reusable objects to prevent waste of potentially useful materials, reduce the consumption of fresh raw materials, energy usage, air pollution (from incineration) and water pollution (from landfilling) by decreasing the need for "conventional" waste disposal and lowering greenhouse gas emissions compared to plastic production.

Recycling is a key component of modern waste reduction and is the third component of the "Reduce, Reuse and Recycle" waste hierarchy. "

The Benefits of Recycling

Environmental Benefits

1. By recycling, people can prevent millions of tons of material from entering landfills, saving space for garbage that cannot be repurposed.

There are over 1,500 landfill sites in the UK, which produced a quarter of the UK's emissions of methane, a powerful greenhouse gas. Landfills not only pollute the environment but also hamper the beauty of the city.

2. Recycling reduces the need for extracting (mining, quarrying and logging), refining and processing raw materials, all of which create substantial air and water pollution. The pollutants that are released into the air and water can be greatly reduced with an increase in recycling.

3. As recycling saves energy, it also reduces greenhouse gas emissions, which helps to tackle climate change. Recent UK recycling is estimated to save more than 18 million tons of CO_2 a year, equivalent to taking 5 million cars off the road. In short, recycling reduces greenhouse gas emissions into the atmosphere.

4. Using recycled materials in the manufacturing process uses considerably less energy than that required for producing new products from raw materials also when compared

with all associated costs, including transport etc, as these are industry-ready materials. It greatly reduces the amount of energy used daily by not needing to produce new materials.

5. When we recycle, used materials are converted into new products, reducing the need to consume natural resources. If used materials are not recycled, new products are made by extracting fresh, raw material from the Earth, through mining and forestry.

Recycling helps conserve the Earth's natural resources like raw materials, minerals, trees, etc. It protects natural habitats for the future and preserves natural resources for future generations.

6. If for absolutely nothing else, recycling keeps litter overflow to a minimum keeping the Earth looking beautiful.

7. In terms of energy, a single light bulb can be powered for up to four hours with the energy saved from one recycled glass bottle.

Economic Benefits

1. Recycling contributes to a circular economy where everything is a resource rather than waste. Properly run recycling programs cost the government, taxpayers, and business owners less money than waste programs.

2. Studies show that by continuing to increase positive recycling habits, the United States can create over one million jobs annually. For every one job created in the waste management industry, recycling creates four.

3. People can even make money by collecting approved materials to a nearby recycling facility that will pay for the product.

4. It is cheaper than waste collection and disposal. Lambeth council in London pointed out in 2017 that "it is 6 times cheaper to dispose of recycled waste than general refuse."

So, the more you recycle, and the less you put in the bin, the more money is saved to use for households, businesses and local public services.

5. When materials are recycled locally, it boosts your local economy by creating more jobs in the recycling process and creates a better future for all.

Your recycling efforts also create new businesses like collection, transportation, processing, manufacturing, packaging and selling of recycled products, paving the way for a greener future.

6. Recycling can boost the tourism industry of countries. A clean environment is welcoming and would attract environmental enthusiasts around the world. This influx of tourists would also contribute to the foreign exchange reserve of a country.

Circular Economy and Recycling

For a long time, our economy has been 'linear'. This means that raw materials are used to make a product, and after its use any waste (e.g. packaging) is thrown away. In an economy based on recycling, materials are reused. For example, waste glass is used to make new glass and waste paper is used to make new paper. To ensure that in the future there are enough raw materials for food, shelter, heating and other necessities, our economy must become circular. That means preventing waste by making products and materials more efficiently and reusing them. If new raw materials are needed, they must be obtained sustainably so that the natural and human environment is not damaged.

From a linear to a circular economy

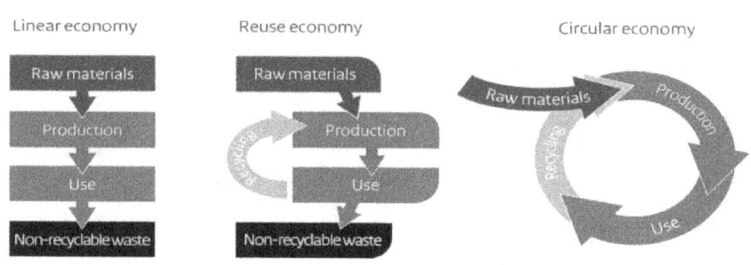

What is Circular Economy?

In a circular economy, manufacturers design products to be reusable. For example, electrical devices are designed in such a way that they are easier to repair. Products and raw materials are also reused as much as possible. For example, by recycling plastic into pellets for making new plastic products. In a circular economy we treat our surroundings responsibly. For example, by preventing litter on streets or in the natural environment.

Recycling begins at the end - the 'get rid' stage of a product's lifecycle. The circular economy, however, goes right back to the beginning to prevent waste and pollution from being created in the first place. In the face of our current environmental challenges, recycling won't be enough to overcome the sheer amount of waste we produce.

"In a properly built circular economy, one should rather focus on avoiding the recycling stage at all costs. It may sound straightforward, but preventing waste from being created in the first place is the only realistic strategy." World Economic Forum

Recycling is a necessary component of a circular economy, though should only be considered when there are no other alternatives for re-use, remanufacture or repair. This is the basic premise of the waste hierarchy (Reduce, re-use, recycle), which prioritizes the most effective solutions to waste management.

Steps to Recycling Materials

Recycling includes the three steps below, which create a continuous loop, represented by the familiar recycling symbol.

Step 1: Collection and Processing

There are several methods for collecting recyclables, including curbside collection, drop-off centers, and deposit or refund programs.

After collection, recyclables are sent to a recovery facility to be sorted, cleaned and processed into materials that can be used in manufacturing. Recyclables are bought and sold just like raw materials would be, and prices go up and down depending on supply and demand in the United States and the world.

Step 2: Manufacturing

More and more of today's products are being manufactured with recycled content. Common household items that contain recycled materials include the following:

- Newspapers and paper towels

- Aluminum, plastic, and glass soft drink containers

- Steel cans

- Plastic laundry detergent bottles

Recycled materials are also used in new ways such as recovered glass in asphalt to pave roads or recovered plastic in carpeting and park benches.

Step 3: Purchasing New Products Made from Recycled Materials

You help close the recycling loop by buying new products made from recycled materials. There are thousands of products that contain recycled content. (US EPA, 2020)

The Three Types of Recycling

1. Mechanical Recycling

One of the most globally used methods of giving residues new usages is mechanic recycling. This method is used to recycle plastics, either obtained from industrial scrap, or domestic, or commercial disposals. The residues are mechanically transformed into new materials without changing their chemical structures.

Mechanical recycling is the process of making plastic wastes useful by processes like grinding, washing, separating, drying, re-granulating, and compounding. The polymers stay unaffected in this process and can be reused again and again in the same or similar product. Such mechanically recycled plastics are used in making garbage bags, floors, hoses, car parts, and packages. Mechanical recycling is widely used for Polyolefin (PE and PP).

2. Energy Recycling

The method used to convert plastics into both thermal and electric energy is called energy recycling. The process is done by leveraging, through incineration and the heat is released in the form of fuel. As this recycling process requires a little room, it can diversify the energetic matrix and optimize the space available in highly populated cities. As it is not financially sustainable, so it requires heavy investment and public authorities' engagement. This recycling method is widely used in Europe and Japan.

Furthermore, energy recycling is an environmental-friendly solution. There are catalyzers in waste incineration plants to withhold the emissions of the energy recycling process. Miguel Bahiense, Plastivida's CEO, the Social and Environmental Institute for Plastics says that:

"In the '70s and '80s, energy recycling was considered negatively as its emissions had adverse effects on the environment. Now the incineration equipment has become advanced and makes sure that emissions are environment-friendly."

3. Chemical Recycling

Among all types of recycling, chemical recycling is the most complex method. In this process, the chemical structures of plastics are modified after reprocessing them. The final product is produced to be used as raw material in different industries. It can also be used as a basic input in manufacturing new plastic products. It is an expensive process and requires a large amount of plastic available.

According to Miguel Bahiense, Plastivida's CEO, the chemical recycling process is still under development. So it's too early to talk about its potential. Chemical recycling instead of replacing energy and mechanical methods, proposes alternative solutions to these processes". He said "Chemical recycling process exists only in labs and we can't refer to it as a real-world thing. This process is still in its early development stages. It is a complex process and requires great technology development."

Recyclable Materials

Paper: These plant-derived materials are commonly recycled, but have different grades. Paper cannot be recycled if it is wet, has food contamination, or has been recycled multiple times already. There are three grades of paper used for making recycled products.

1. Cardboard (OCC)

2. Office paper

3. Newsprint / magazines

Glass: This is a (mostly) transparent solid material that is mostly used for practical and decorative applications. It comes in three different colors, all used in different applications, which are all widely recyclable.

- Amber – used frequently for beer bottles

- Green – occasionally used for beer bottles.

- Clear – often used for food/beverage packaging or for more practical and decorative needs

E-Waste: These materials include some type of electronic component and are most often disassembled in order to be recycled.

Textiles: These are fabrics and typically make up clothing or accessories.

Batteries: Despite having a chemical and electrical component, some batteries can be recycled.

Plastics (by Recycling Code): While these symbols appear on many items to identify recyclability, they do not necessary means that the items are recyclable. For instance, a #1 (PET) is very commonly recycled while a #7 (Other) cannot be recycled in many places. Here is a breakdown of the recycling codes and what they all mean:

- #1 PET – This is a type of plastic commonly used in water bottles, blister packs, and clear food packaging.

- #2 HDPE – This is a type of higher-melting plastic that is used in milk jugs, cleaning solution bottles, trigger bottles, etc.

- #3 PVC – This type of plastic is used in the white pipes/tubes that most modern plumbing is made with.

- #4 LDPE – This is a type of lower-melting plastic that makes up your shopping bag and some stretch wrap.

- #5 PP – This is a type of higher-melting plastic used for dairy tubs, the caps on most bottles, and things like storage containers.

- #6 PS – This plastic is used to make styrofoam food containers, disposable dining utensils, and yogurt containers.

- #7 Other – This category refers to everything else that does not fall into the previous six, or a combination of any of the previous items used together in a single product. Some other types of plastics that fall into this category are:

  - ABS – This polymer is often used to make the rigid plastic housings for electronics, remotes, toys, and more.

  - PA (Nylon) – This plastic is often used in fabrics, plastic zip or cable ties, and other industrial parts.

Metals:

- Aluminum – Aluminum is one of the most common metals on the planet, and its properties make it important for many products and their packaging. This is one of the most important materials to recycle.

- Steel - This is a common metal for durable goods and load-bearing objects. Examples of product applications that use steel include metal appliances, cars, and load-bearing beams.

- Copper – Copper is used in electrical applications and electronic products due to its excellent thermal and electrical conductivity. (Terracycle, 2021)

Common Recyclable Items in everyday life

There are so many materials that can be recycled in today's society; it would take a book to go into detail about each and every one. Listed below, however, are some of the most common recyclable items people come across in their everyday lives.

1. Metal

Metals that we use in our everyday life are often times recyclable. Being a very versatile material, recycling metal takes more than seventy percent less energy than it does to produce a completely new item.

Aluminum foil – (As well as bake ware) can easily be recycled. By melting down the foil products and simply repurposing, the metal aluminum can be recycled almost infinitely.

Aluminum cans – Studies show that Americans drink at least one canned beverage per day while only recycling a little over forty-five percent. It would save immense amounts of energy to recycle and reuse them as opposed to making new ones.

Steel and tin cans – Things like coffee cans, soup containers, vegetable cans, etc. are one of the most recycled materials in America. This is a comforting statistic considering, on average, about 100 million are used daily in the States.

2. Paper and Cardboard

Most people can look around themselves at just about any point in the day and see paper or paper products. Paper is a material that has no limits in the recycling world, and Americans are doing a great job in recycling. Studies show that people are recycling about 334 pounds of paper annually. Paper and cardboard materials that can be recycled are:

Corrugated cardboard – This makes up most of the cardboard in people's everyday lives, over seventy percent of shipping boxes already having been repurposed from sawdust, woodchips, or other paper products. Other items recycled cardboard is used to make are things like cereal boxes, tissue paper, printing paper, and poster board.

Magazines and newspapers – Many people still get magazines and newspapers on their mailboxes and their front porches. Too frequently, these are junk ads or unwanted publications that go directly into the trash. One ton of recycled paper can save enough energy to power an American household for over five months.

Office paper and poster board – Most people interact with at least one piece of paper a day. Papers are in the mailbox, printer, and briefcase next to the door, everywhere. Paper can be easily repurposed, saving high production costs and energy levels for new products.

3. Glass

Glass bottles and jars are not quite as versatile as paper or metal products when it comes to recycling. Due to the various colors of glass, many items can only be repurposed into another of the same item. The different types of glass recycling typically pertain to the color of the bottle or jar.

Flint glass – This is the term used to refer to clear glass items, which make up the largest part of the glass market at just over sixty percent. Usually, items bottled in clear glass containers are not light-sensitive, and people want to have seen.

Amber glass – One of the reasons glass can be hard to recycle is due to the fact that the colors cannot be removed. For instance, amber, or brown, glass makes up less of the glass market than flint at thirty-one percent partially because it can only be made into other amber-colored glass products when recycled. Generally, items that are sensitive to sunlight are stored in brown colored glass bottles and jars.

Emerald glass – When one thinks emerald, or green, glass wine and beer bottles typically come to mind. This is because the items inside are sensitive to sunlight and temperature, however not quite as sensitive as products that need to be stored in brown glass containers.

4. Plastics (PET)

The clear plastic water and beverage bottles or plastic make up about 95% of this category. Clear plastic cups and packaging, such as on retail products, accounts for the remaining 5%. It is a popular recycling program; however, plastics recycling are not as successful as the other leading materials.

PET (polyethylene terephthalate) is clear plastic water and beverage bottles.

HDPE plastic, (High Density Polyethylene), or PEHD is a thermoplastic polymer produced from the monomer ethylene, and non-clear plastic, such as those opaque milk jugs, shampoo bottles, or other colored plastics.

Other "colored plastics" such as straws to bottle caps, plastic spoons to Red Solo cups, and Legos to rubber duckies. High density plastics include almost all stiff or flexible plastic items.

5. Electronic or "E-Waste"

Electronic gadgets contain chemicals and metals that can be hazardous if they're thrown into a landfill. We can do a little research to determine which local facilities will accept and recycle them. These items can be

Computers

Stereos

Cell phones and batteries

Old televisions

Old household items

6. Other Items

Concrete – It typically only comes from construction and demolition waste.

Steel – Domestic steel scrap is used in the production of new steel.

Countries with the Best Recycling Rates

Using data from the latest report by Eunomia and the European Environmental Bureau (EEB) from 2017, combined with stats from the United Nations Statistics Division (UNSD), these are the best 5 countries in recycling rates.

1. Germany – 66.1%

Germany has the best recycling rate in the world; it leads the way with 66.1% of its waste being recycled. It has six different bins: black for general waste, blue for paper, yellow for plastic, white for clear glass, green for colored glass and brown for composting. This means that citizens must do the sorting themselves, which reduces the amount of money the government has to spend on sorting, as well as reducing contamination. German law makes companies responsible for making their packaging reusable or recyclable, operating under a 'polluter pays' principle and all recyclable items are marked with a recognizable green dot.

2. Wales – 63.8%

In second place is Wales, recycling an impressive 63.8% of its waste, which leaves neighboring England lagging behind with its 42.8% recycling rate. Wales was the first UK nation to start charging for plastic bags, in 2011, resulting in a 70% drop in their use. The country's success in increasing its recycling has been attributed to setting statutory targets, improving separate waste collection services and engaging communities to recycle.

3. Singapore - 61%

Singapore's high recycling rates owe more to informal recyclers – known as karung guni – than they do to the government's National Recycling Programme. The karung guni collected around 20% of all household recyclable waste in 2016, while the national recycling effort collected just 2%. These informal collectors visit households and pick up all types of recyclable waste, including electronics, which they sell on to dealers and recycling companies.

4. South Korea – 59%

South Korea is another country that's turned its recycling reputation around – particularly when it comes to food waste. Back in 1995, a mere 2% of food waste was recycled, while today that figure has risen to 95% according to a study published in the Journal of Material Cycles and Waste Management. Since 2013, Seoul residents have been legally required to dispose of food waste in biodegradable bags. They are charged a small fee for the bags, which is intended to discourage food wastage, and the fees pay for the cost of collecting and processing the city's waste. Pictured are food waste bins in Seoul.

5. Taiwan – 58%

Taiwan has an offbeat way of encouraging people to recycle – its garbage collection trucks blast classical music to remind people to bring their bins out. But it's clearly working. In 1993, virtually nothing was recycled and only 70% of overall trash was collected, lending it the nickname of "Garbage Island". Today, the country reports an impressive 58% recycling rate. Other initiatives that have helped include composting of raw food waste, which is turned into fertilizer, and fines for not disposing of waste correctly.

Global and International Recycling Organizations

The Bureau of International Recycling (BIR)	
Description	The Bureau of International Recycling (BIR) is the only global recycling industry federation representing around 800 companies and 35 affiliated national recycling associations from 70 different countries. Its members are world leaders in the supply of raw materials and a key pillar for sustainable economic development. **There are 4 Saudi Members in the Bureau:** 1- Rayanco Saudia Trading Co. LTD. 2- Al-Qaryan Group for Trading, Industry and Contracting 3- Alsaggaff Trading EST 4- Mametals Press Scrap CO
Website	https://www.bir.org/
Contact Details	24 Avenue Franklin Roosevelt, 1050 Brussels, Belgium Tel: +32 2 627 57 70 E-mail: bir@bir.org
Global Recycling Foundation	
Description	The Global Recycling Foundation supports the promotion of recycling, and the recycling industry, across the world to showcase its vital role in preserving the future of the planet. It was formed in October 2018 as **a private Foundation**. Its mission is to fund educational and awareness programs, innovation initiatives which focus on the sustainable and inclusive development of recycling, across the world.
Website	https://www.globalrecyclingfoundation.org/
Contact Details	E-mail: info@globalrecyclingfoundation.org
The Zero Waste International Alliance (ZWIA)	
Description	The Zero Waste International Alliance is the internationally recognized online source for Zero Waste standards, policies and best practices for communities and businesses. The Zero Waste International Alliance has recognized nonprofit organizations, municipalities, and businesses across the globe as

	leaders working towards zero waste.
Website	https://zwia.org/zero-waste-organizations/
Contact Details	Contact Person: Richard Anthony (Chair) Address: 3891 Kendall Street, San Diego, CA, 92109 United States of America

The International Solid Waste Association **ISWA**	
Description	The International Solid Waste Association is an international network of waste professionals and experts from around the world whose mission is "To Promote and Develop Sustainable and Professional Waste Management Worldwide and the transition to a circular economy."
Website	https://www.iswa.org/?v=fbe46383db39
Contact Details	Stationsplein 45 A4.004, 3013 AK Rotterdam The Netherlands E-mail: iswa@iswa.org Tel: +31 (0)10 808 3990

Sustainable Electronics Recycling International **SERI**	
Description	SERI is the only multi-stakeholder, collaborative **nonprofit organization** in the world focused exclusively on minimizing the environmental and health risks posed by used and end-of-life electronics, while also maximizing the social and economic value presented by this equipment. Solving the world's electronics sustainability problem is going to take committed individuals, businesses, policy makers, and institutions all working together. SERI's role is to bring all those disparate parts together to bring about real change.
Website	https://sustainableelectronics.org/
Contact Details	Online form: https://sustainableelectronics.org/contact-us/

Institute of Scrap Recycling Industries, Inc. **ISRI**	
Description	The Institute of Scrap Recycling Industries (ISRI) is a United States-based private, **non-profit trade association** representing more than 1,300 private and public for-profit companies – ranging from small, family-owned businesses to multi-national corporations—operating at more than 6,000 facilities in the United States and 40 countries worldwide.

	ISRI advocates for safety and responsibility in many different areas of the scrap recycling industry – metals theft, electronics recycling, occupational safety and regulatory compliance of its members. The organization also publishes periodic research on the recycling industry.
Website	**ISRI Websites** ISRI.org ISRISafety.org ISRI2022.org RecycledRubberFacts.org RIOSCertification.org Scrap.org ScrapTheftAlert.com StopMetalsTheft.org
Contact Details	Institute of Scrap Recycling Industries, Inc. 1250 H Street, NW Suite 400 Washington, DC 20005 Phone: (202) 662-8500 Fax: (202) 624-9256
Bureau of Middle East Recycling **BMR**	
Description	The BMR was formed as **a non-profit** oriented, non-religious, non-political organization to mainly represent all the suppliers/traders of the Middle East Recycling Industry and to bring them under one banner and platform with the unified thoughts of promoting the Metal Recycling Business of Middle East, protecting the environment and sharing market information about metal recycling and to face the new challenges in the present financial crises. This bureau is focused mainly on Unity among Middle East Recycling Industry which is one of the largest geographical sectors dealing with million tons of scrap which yields billions of US dollars. Recycling commodities: ferrous, non-ferrous, paper, e-waste, plastic
Website	http://bmr.ae/home.html
Contact Details	Landline No. +971 4 437 5744/ +971 4 431 4614[Fax No.] Address: Bureau of Middle East Recycling 16th Floor, Jumeirah Bay X2 Tower, X cluster, Jumeirah Lakes Towers Dubai, United Arab Emirates.

The World's Biggest Recycling Companies

The platform "Insider Monkey" listed the biggest companies, whose main business is recycling, worldwide. The rankings are based on the companies' average revenue per year. Where available, they used the actual financial statements of the company, and converted them to USD for a standard metric in case the company is foreign.

Waste Management, Inc. United States	
Description	Waste Management tops the list of the 5 biggest recycling companies in the world. Founded in 1968 in Chicago, Illinois, Waste Management (NYSE: WM) is a waste management, comprehensive waste, and environmental services company in North America. Its headquarters are in Houston, Texas in the First City Tower. It operates 293 active landfill disposals and 146 recycling plants, as well as 111 beneficial-use landfill gas projects and six independent power production plants. Waste Management generates annual revenue of 14.48 billion USD. **Materials they recycle:** WM makes safe, responsible disposal and recycling of old bulbs, batteries and other **"hard to dispose of" items.** They also pick up and responsibly dispose household **hazardous waste** such as paints, chemicals, automotive products and more.
Website	https://www.wm.com/us/en
Veolia Environmental Services (Private) **France**	
Description	With 29 billion USD in yearly revenue, Veolia Environmental makes the list of the biggest recycling companies in the world. The company was founded in 1853 and is headquartered in Paris, France. Veolia Environmental provides services in management, treatment and disposal of waste, in addition to recycling, reclamation and re-use of waste products. The company has its presence in 35 countries and employees nearly 70,000 employees. **Materials they recycle:** Radioactive waste, hazardous waste, hazardous chemicals, sensitive products and confidential documents.
Website	https://www.veolia.com/en
Republic Services, Inc. **United States**	
Description	The second largest recycling company in the United States, Republic Services (NYSE: RSG) is based in Arizona. Its services include non-hazardous solid waste collection, transfer, disposal, recycling, and

	energy services. It generates an average of 9.4 billion USD per year. **Materials they recycle:** Non-hazardous solid waste.
Website	https://www.republicservices.com/

Waste Connections, Inc. **United States**	
Description	Waste Connections (NYSE: WCN) was founded in 1997 in Texas, United States. The company provides waste collection, transfer, disposal and recycling services, primarily of solid waste. Its headquarters are in The Woodlands, Texas and Vaughan, Ontario as it operates in Canada as well. It is one of North America's third largest waste management companies. Waste Connections generates yearly revenue of 4.92 Billion USD. **Materials they recycle:** Non-hazardous solid waste.
Website	https://www.wasteconnections.com/

Clean Harbors, Inc. **United Kingdom**	
Description	Founded in 1980 in Norwell, United Kingdom, Clean Harbors is a provider of environmental, energy and industrial services. It also provides hazardous waste disposal services to companies, small waste generators and federal, state, provincial and local governments. It has over 400 service locations throughout North America, Canada and Puerto Rico. Clean Harbors generates a yearly revenue of 3.4 billion USD. **Materials they recycle:** hazardous and non-hazardous waste.
Website	https://www.cleanharbors.com/

GFL Environmental Inc. **Canada**	
Description	GFL Environmental is one of the biggest Canadian recycling companies. The company was founded just 14 years ago in 2007. According to its 20-F filing, "GFL is the fourth largest diversified environmental services company in North America, with operations throughout Canada and in 27 states in the United States. GFL had more than 15,000 employees as of December 31, 2020." Revenue of the company in 2019 (in millions of dollars): 3347 **Materials they recycle:** residential solid waste, Commercial solid waste, and Commercial liquid and special waste.

Website	https://gflenv.com/

Stericycle, Inc. United States	
Description	SRCL ranks 7th on the list of the biggest recycling companies in the world. The company is headquartered in Illinois and was founded back in 1989. The company is one of the few recycling companies in our list to have actually made a loss in 2019. And we'll just have to wait for the 2020 annual report to see if the company has successfully maneuvered one of the most difficult years in history. Revenue of the company in 2019 (in millions of dollars): 3,309 **Materials they recycle:** hazardous, bio-hazardous, sharp, and chemotherapy waste.
Website	https://www.stericycle.com/en-us

Renewi plc United Kingdom	
Description	Founded in 1880, Renewi plc. is headquartered in Milton Keynes, United Kingdom. The leading European waste management company primarily operates in the Benelux region. It was originally founded as a construction company in the west of Scotland. It changed its status from a construction company to a waste management company in the mid 1990's. Renewi plc. generates an annual revenue of 2.1 billion USD. **Materials they recycle:** glass, paper and cards, rubble recycling and water treatment.
Website	https://www.renewi.com/en/

Covanta Energy Corporation United States	
Description	CVA ranks 9th on the list of the biggest recycling companies in the world. Coventa Energy Corporation was found in 1939 in New Jersey, United States. It provides services in energy from waste conversion and industrial waste management. The company charges a fee for waste disposal, sells electricity produced in the process, and recovers metal for recycling. Coventa generates an annual revenue of 1.8 billion USD. **Materials they recycle:** total waste, liquid, plastic, hard, pharmaceutical, electronic, and medical waste.
Website	https://www.covanta.com/

	Cleanaway Waste Management Limited **Australia**
Description	The Australian waste management company is headquartered in Melbourne. It was founded in 1979 and generates a yearly revenue of 2.1 billion USD. The company has over 250 branches throughout the country and employs over 6000 people. Cleanaway Waste Management Limited operates over 5,300 trucks. **Materials they recycle:** hazardous and non-hazardous waste.
Website	https://www.cleanaway.com.au/

	Biffa plc **United Kingdom**
Description	Biffa ranks 11th on the list of the biggest recycling companies in the world. Based in High Wycombe, United Kingdom, Biffa was found in 1912. The waste management company provides services in collection, landfill, recycling and special waste services to local authorities and industrial and commercial clients. It is noted to be the United Kingdom's second largest waste management company as of 2017. The company generates annual revenue of 1.4 billion USD. **Materials they recycle:** asbestos, food and general waste.
Website	https://www.biffa.co.uk/

	Recology (Private) **United States**
Description	The Californian company is headquartered in San Francisco, and offers a ton of services which include waste management and reclaiming usable materials, while also operating several landfills. Revenue of the company in 2019 (in millions of dollars): 1,300 **Materials they recycle:** yard trimmings and food scraps.
Website	https://www.recology.com/about-us/

	US Ecology, Inc. **United States**
Description	US Ecology proclaims to be an industry leader in environmental services, and its revenue seems to back that up. The company offers the proper disposal of both hazardous as well as non-hazardous waste, and even radioactive waste. Not only does the company treat the waste, it also works on recycling them as well. Revenue of the company in 2019 (in millions of dollars): 1,051 **Materials they recycle:** solid waste, hazardous waste, radioactive

	waste, energy waste, and wastewater treatment.
Website	https://www.usecology.com/

Casella Waste Systems, Inc. **United States**	
Description	CWST ranks 14th on our list of the biggest recycling companies in the world. The company is headquartered in Vermont, and has at least 2,300 employees. It is one of the older companies in our list, having been founded back in 1975 and is considered to be a vertically integrated waste management and recycling company. The company has acquired a market capitalization of at least $3 billion, which is a great achievement for any company. Revenue of the company in 2019 (in millions of dollars): 743 **Materials they recycle:** general, solid and medical waste
Website	https://www.casella.com/

Bingo Industries Limited **Australia**	
Description	Based in New South Wales, Australia, Bingo Industries is a waste management and recycling company founded in 2005. It was founded and is headed by the Tartak Family, with Daniel Tartak being the current CEO. The company operates residential and commercial recycling and waste services as well as bin manufacturing services through its subsidiaries. Revenue of the company in 2019 (in millions of dollars): 398 **Materials they recycle:** general and commercial waste, from hazardous waste and contaminated soils to cardboard and concrete.
Website	https://www.bingoindustries.com.au/

The World's Biggest Recycling Nonprofits

WasteAid UK	
Description	WasteAid is an independent UK **charity (non-profit),** set up by waste management professionals to share practical and low-cost waste management know-how with communities in low-income countries. WasteAid was set up in 2015 to share know-how and skills with communities that can benefit from this type of advice and support.
Website	https://wasteaid.org/
Contact Details	Phone: +44 (0) 1233 877273 UK office address: 8 Zealds House, 39 Church St, Wye, Kent TN25 5BL Facebook: https://facebook.com/wasteaid Twitter: https://twitter.com/wasteaid LinkedIn: https://www.linkedin.com/company/10272657

WRAP UK	
Description	WRAP was established as **a not-for-profit** company in 2000; and became a charity in 2014. WRAP is one of the globe's leading sustainability charities. Based in the UK and with projects around the world we work with businesses, governments, citizens and charities to make the planet a healthier, safer place. We promote and encourage sustainable resource use through product design, waste minimization, re-use, recycling and reprocessing of waste materials. They are sprcialized in 4 main areas: **Food and drink, Plastic packaging, Clothing and textiles, and Collections and recycling**
Website	https://wrap.org.uk/
Contact Details	Tel: 01295 819900 Address: WRAP, Second Floor, Blenheim Court, 19 George Street, Banbury OX16 5BH England Enquiry Form: https://wrap.org.uk/contact-us

	YouTube: https://www.youtube.com/user/ResourceEfficiency
	Twitter: https://twitter.com/WRAP_UK
	LinkedIn: https://www.linkedin.com/company/215390

National Recycling Coalition NRC
United States

Description	The National Recycling Coalition is **a non-profit organization** focused on promoting and enhancing recycling in the United States. Our network of more than 6,000 members extends across waste reduction, reuse, recycling, and composting. Together, We Are Recycling. The Mission of the National Recycling Coalition is to partner with and facilitate activities between and among non-profit organizations (NGO's), businesses, trade associations, individuals and government to maintain a prosperous and productive American recycling system that is committed to the conservation of natural resources.
Website	https://nrcrecycles.org/
Contact Details	SUNY College of Environmental Science and Forestry 1 Forestry Drive, 203 Bray Hall Syracuse, NY 13210 nrcexecdirector@gmail.com

National Center for Electronics Recycling (NCER)
United States

Description	The National Center for Electronics Recycling (NCER) is **a non-profit organization** formed in 2005 that is dedicated to the development and enhancement of a national infrastructure for the recycling of used electronics in the U.S.
Website	https://www.electronicsrecycling.org/
Contact Details	Phone: 304-699-1008. E-mail: jlinnell@electronicsrecycling.org

The North America Hazardous Materials Management Association (NAHMMA),
United States

Description	Established in 1993, the North American Hazardous Materials Management Association (NAHMMA) is the premier association for professionals working to reduce and manage household hazardous waste. A volunteer-run, **non-profit organization**, NAHMMA is

	committed to pollution prevention, product stewardship, and the safe and effective handling of hazardous materials from households and small businesses. NAHMMA supports its members with exclusive training opportunities, relevant industry news, and access to a diverse and experienced nationwide network of people involved in the hazardous waste management industry.
Website	https://nahmma.org/
Contact Details	Facebook: https://www.facebook.com/NAHMMA/posts/ LinkedIn: https://www.linkedin.com/company/nahmma

Recycling and Waste Management Publications

Recycling International – Recycling International is written specifically for the global recycling industries and features many case studies. Website: https://recyclinginternational.com/magazine/
Waste Advantage Magazine Website: https://wasteadvantagemag.com/
Global Recycling – Magazine of global trends in the circular economy, particularly in the recycling and recovery industry as well as in waste recycling. Markets for technology, logistics and raw materials. Website: https://global-recycling.info/
Recycling Magazine – Recycling Magazine is a top recycling industry publication for her German speaking countries, but the site is also available to read in English. Website: https://www.recycling-magazine.com/
Recycling Today (RT) and Recycling Today Global Edition (RTGE) – RT provides broad coverage of the recycling industry and offers an in-depth view of market and commodity information along with news, industry developments and company profiles of recyclers. Website: https://www.recyclingtoday.com/magazine/
Environmental Expert – Environmental XPRT is a global environmental industry marketplace and information resource. Website: http://www.environmental-expert.com/
Let's Recycle – Let's Recycle reaches the waste management and recycling sector, local authorities and UK commerce and industry. Website: https://www.letsrecycle.com/
Materials Recycling World (MRW) – MRW is a UK based business resource and website in the recycling and waste management industry. Website: https://www.mrw.co.uk/
Recycling and Waste World – Recycling and Waste World is a UK based weekly

newspaper dedicated to the recycling and waste management industries.   Website: https://www.recyclingwasteworld.co.uk/
Resource – Resource is a UK based publication for the "waste to resource" industry.   Website: https://resource.co/
Resource Recycling – Resource Recycling's publications focus extensively on the latest recycling trends, market analysis, research, equipment and business news for the recycling and waste management industry.   Website: https://resource-recycling.com/
Waste Management World – WMW provides news for the waste management industry in the UK.   Website: https://waste-management-world.com/

Recycling Ideas and Initiatives from Around the Globe

The Nonprofit that Transforms Flip-flop Flotsam into Art

Ocean Sole, a Kenyan Solution to Sea Pollution

Around 8.8 million tons of plastic enter the ocean each year. Soda bottles, grocery bags, and six-pack rings aren't the only plastic items polluting the world's waterways and harming fish, turtles, and other animals: In 1997, marine conservationist Julie Church came across a beach in Kenya that was strewn with discarded flip-flops.

Church noticed children making toys from the debris, and convinced local women to collect, wash, and process the flip-flops into colorful art objects. This initiative grew into **Ocean Sole**; a fair-trade business that today collects flip-flop flotsam from Kenya's beaches and waters and transforms them into plastic sculptures, accessories, and trinkets. Ocean Sole's goal is to recycle 750,000 flip-flops per year, and the organization also provides business opportunities to women living in city slums and remote coastal areas.

Website: https://oceansoleonline.com/

The Ecological Nonprofit that Collects Hair to Clean up Oil Spills

Work at a beauty salon or own a furry pet? Instead of tossing shorn or shed hair into the trash, donate it to **Matter of Trust**. The San Francisco-based ecological charity's **Clean Wave program** collects hair and fur, and uses it to make oil-absorbing mats and stuff containment booms. Hazmat teams use these all-natural tools to clean up after oil spills, and public works departments use them to keep motor oil drip spills out of waterways.

In addition to large-scale donations from beauty salons, barbershops, and groomers, Matter of Trust also accepts smaller contributions from private individuals. If you're interested in helping out, visit Matter of Trust's website, register to participate in the nonprofit's Excess Access recycling program, and follow the instructions to donate. The program's need for hair and fur ebbs and flows, depending on the volume of recent donations. But in the case of an emergency oil spill, all donations are welcome. (Cases in point: Matter of Trust's hair mats and booms were used to help clean up after both the 2007 Cosco Busan oil spill in the San Francisco Bay and the 2010 BP Deep water Horizon oil spill in the Gulf of Mexico.)

Website: https://matteroftrust.org/clean-wave-program/

The Nonprofit that Re-purposes Old Crayons into New Ones

As art supplies go, crayons are relatively cheap, making it all too easy and inexpensive to toss scuzzy, broken, and worn-down wax stubs into the trash and purchase new ones. But crayons are typically made from paraffin wax and aren't biodegradable—so to keep old art tools from clogging landfills, a Northern California-based nonprofit called **The Crayon Initiative** collects unwanted crayons from restaurants and schools and melts them down to make fresh ones. Then, they donate the re-purposed goods to children's hospitals. Family restaurants and schools can find out how to organize crayon donation drives online.

Website: https://thecrayoninitiative.org/

A Company that makes Recycling a Rewarding Habit with "Reverse Vending Machines"

Most people acknowledge that recycling is an important path toward circularity, but who knew it could also be fun? Norwegian company **TOMRA** aims to make recycling a rewarding habit with reverse vending machines, which gives users credit in exchange for depositing used drinks containers. Over 84,000 of these machines are scattered across the globe, capturing an estimated 40 billion drinks containers every year.

Additionally, this year, TOMRA and its partners are kicking off operations at a new advanced mechanical recycling plant in Lahnstein, Germany. This facility will produce high-purity polymers suitable for demanding applications, such as in automotive manufacturing.

TOMRA shows it takes a multi-pronged approach to help end plastic waste, boosting both the recycling industry's capabilities while working to shift consumer behavior toward sustainability.

Website: https://www.tomra.com/en/collection/reverse-vending

"Grow Recycling" a preschool kids game about recycling

Gro Recycling is a preschool kid's game about recycling that is fun, but also a great way for kids and parents to learn about recycling and taking care of our planet's resources. Kids feed the recycling bins their garbage to find out which characters like which recyclables. Then trash is made into new products that the players sorted with the recycling machines. Right now, grow Recycling is used in sustainability education by thousands of schools and preschools in the USA and Europe.

"iRecycle" Recycling App by Earth911 Organization

Earth911 – an organization that helps people all over the world learn more about recycling by providing ideas that are easy to implement. To spread this initiative further, they created the iRecycle app, which helps Americans find accessible recycling venues in their areas, and suggests a million different ways to recycle materials. It has one of the largest recycling databases in the world. It has a well-designed search directory that allows users to look up products of all types, from automotive to household items, and provides relevant information regarding the drop-off point such as location address, phone number and opening hours. The iRecycle app also offers news section that provides the latest information with regards to the waste and recycling sectors.

Kenya's Recycled Pencils, MOMO Pencils Green Manufacturing Company

Globally, we get through 14 billion pencils each year, with a lot of wood going into their manufacture. A few years ago, Kenyan entrepreneurs began producing eco-friendly, non-toxic pencils from recycled newspaper. Their bright idea has quickly progressed from rough sketch to thriving business, supplying schools, government agencies and corporate firms.

Website: https://momopencils.com/

Turning Tires into Cushions in Niger

Niger's capital Niamey has no regular rubbish collection so trash is often burned at illegal dumping sites. Environmental activist Amina Issa Ado in Niger hit upon a great way to recycle tires, while at the same time creating jobs for locals: making seat cushions out of used tires. The recycled cushions are also more comfortable and even last longer than traditional Sahel ones.

https://www.livingcircular.veolia.com/en/eco-citizen/amina-issa-ados-sustainable-pouffes

A Nonprofit that Takes Reusable Art and Music Supplies and Redistributes Them

The Dreaming Zebra Foundation takes reusable art and music supplies and redistributes them throughout the world. The Portland, Oregon nonprofit operates on a core belief that all children, regardless of their financial circumstances, should have access to the arts.

Website: https://dreamingzebra.org/

A Nonprofit that Solves Hygiene-related Illness by Collecting and Recycling Soap

Soap is one of the most efficient and cost-effective ways to prevent diarrheal diseases which are responsible for killing 1.8 million people per year, millions of lives that could have been saved by simply having access to soap.

Clean the World is addressing this issue and is on a mission to provide access to soap to countries the hardest hit by these diseases. By partnering with Hotels, Resorts and B & B's all over North America, the charity receives donations of unused soap or other hygiene products and has so far delivered 30 million bars of soap to 100 countries.

Website: https://cleantheworld.org/

A Nonprofit that has Diverted 23.8 million pounds of shoes and clothes from landfills

Soles4Souls operates on the premise that one pair of shoes can provide health hope and opportunity for those living in need all around the globe. Soles4Souls has distributed 30 million pairs of new and used shoes in 127 countries and all 50 states in the U.S. The goal is to Wear Out Poverty by providing short-term relief and long-term solutions.

Since 2006, Soles4Souls has diverted 23.8 million pounds of shoes and clothes from landfills. These shoes and clothes help create economic opportunities for entrepreneurs in developing nations, as a gently used pair of shoes can sell for an average of $10. This additional income provides basic necessities for entrepreneurs and their families.

Website: https://soles4souls.org/

A Nonprofit that Recycles Soccer Balls for Kids

Children in economically depressed regions rarely get the opportunity to play with a conventionally manufactured ball. Instead, they fashion a somewhat decent replica out of a bag stuffed with garbage, old clothing bound with rope or a wad of tightly wrapped banana leaves, but it's really not the same and certainly doesn't bounce as it could. In light of this issue, World Vision has, for years, enabled lucky kiddies to kick their first official 'real' soccer ball courtesy of their "Get a Kick Out of Sharing" initiative and the generous donations of people.

Website: https://www.worldvision.org/

A Nonprofit that Facilitates Food Donation

In the United States, 100 billion pounds of food (or one pound per person daily) is discarded every year due to various issues including poor storage, insect infiltration, cosmetic imperfections, spoilage and simple household/food industry waste. If that's not bad enough, approximately 40 million gardeners in the United States either allow the excess fruits of their labor to decompose on the vine or they compost or discard whatever they can't or don't want to eat. Ample Harvest enables backyard gardeners who have an abundance of extra produce to donate it to local food banks without breaking a sweat, doing something good for the community as well as the planet.

Website: https://ampleharvest.org/

A Nonprofit that Recycles Bicycles

The non-profit organization Recycle-A-Bicycle is more than happy to put any unwanted two wheeler to good use, whether you live in the Big Apple (where they're located) or you choose to mail them your donation. In exchange for your generosity, they bestow all of the newly acquired bikes that are in sound condition with the necessary tweaks to make them run smoothly and appear snazzier. (Those that are beyond help are used for parts and sold at a steep discount to avid bicyclists.) Then, through their Earn-A-Bike program, they allow community youth to score a freebie bike of their choice upon the successful completion of a specified number of volunteer hours.

Website: https://www.recycleabicycle.nyc/

A Nonprofit that Recycles Cell Phones for Soldiers

"Cell Phones for Soldiers" is a nonprofit organization that takes donations in the form of newer or gently-used cell phones, recycles them responsibly and uses the proceeds to fund charitable programs for troops at home and abroad.

Some of these programs include "Minutes that Matter" which provides international calling cards to members serving overseas, sending nearly 1500 calling cards a week to connect troops to their loved ones, and "Helping Heroes Home" which is a grant program that aids returning veterans in need.

Website: https://www.cellphonesforsoldiers.com/

Car Heaven: A Charitable Vehicle Recycling Program

In Canada, the days of leaving an old car to rot in a junkyard are over thanks to Car Heaven. Run by the Automotive Recyclers of Canada, this charity allows people to safely get rid of an old vehicle while supporting a Canadian charity, reducing the environmental impact and supporting local green businesses.

Car Heaven takes old cars and removes any contaminants, operating fluids, tires, and reusable parts then crushes and shreds the unusable portion of the car for material recovery where it is used to create new products like lawnmowers, patio chairs or bicycles. So far the charity has removed 120,000 cars from the road in Canada, equating to a reduction in air Pollution by nearly 5,000 tons!

Website: https://carheaven.ca/

Recycled Greeting Cards

Creating a solution to one of many single-use products that often clutter our houses and end up in landfills, **St. Jude's Ranch for Children** accepts used greeting cards and creates new holiday and all-occasion cards.

The Recycled Cards are available to purchase in packs of 10 for the price of $17 which goes to support different services and programs for abused, neglected and homeless children, young adults and their families.

Website: https://stjudesranch.org/about-us/recycled-card-program/

Furniture Bank

By donating gently used furniture to Furniture Bank instead of hauling it to the dump, it's guaranteed to help the thousands of families and children struggling with poverty that can't afford to furnish their homes.

Between the United States and Canada, Furniture Banks have provided beds, tables and chairs to the previously homeless, unemployed and working poor, battered women and children, immigrants, individuals with mental or physical disabilities, and victims of fire, robbery, and natural disasters. Over 100,000 people are helped annually by the organization.

Website: https://furniturebanks.org/

Books for Africa

If you have old books lying around that need a new home other than the Landfill, why not send them to people in desperate need of literature? Since 1988, Books for Africa has shipped over 34 million books to 49 different countries and more than $2.3 million was raised in the last year to ship the books to the students of Africa.

Website: https://www.booksforafrica.org/

The Best Recycling Projects around the Globe

Recycling Cooking Oil in Barcelona

Authorities in Barcelona have begun handing out so-called 'OliPots' so residents can collect their cooking oil and prevent it from contaminating waterways and clogging up sewers. The pots contain a filter which separates the oil from any remaining food particles. Any type of oils will be accepted as part of the scheme, and the oils will be sent off to be turned into useful products like biofuel.

Recycled Street Furniture in Argentina

In a project commissioned by the recycling company C.Re.S.E., a designer has turned recyclable rubbish into street furniture and other outdoor installations to show people that rubbish like paper, tin, glass, PET, nylon, polystyrene, aluminium, and tetra-brick are valuable materials which can be reused and turned into other items.

C.Re.S.E. is a government-owned recycling company which collects household waste and separates, cleans, and sells it to recycling companies around the country so it can be turned into valuable items.

Recycling Turned into Art in Warsaw

Recycling rates in Poland aren't that great, so an art collective called Luzinterruptus came up with a way of increasing recycling awareness among residents in Warsaw. A thousand coloured plastic bags were scattered across one of the city's squares, and each contained a light bulb. The bags were the same colours as the colours that represent recycling - green for glass, yellow for metal, and blue for paper.

Composting in San Francisco

San Francisco leads the way in reducing waste, and it already diverts more than 72% of its waste from landfill thanks to its excellent recycling scheme. Back in 2009, the city stepped up its waste reduction efforts another notch by introducing mandatory composting, passing a law which was the first of its kind in the US. Now residents must put all their organic waste in green composting bins which are stationed all over the city.

Reverse Vending Machines in the US

Residents in North Carolina can take their empty bottles and cans to 'Dream Machines' across the state and they get points and prizes in return. The scheme was created by Pepsi, Keep America Beautiful, and waste management companies, and it's hoped that the machines will help people to recycle when they don't have access to a recycling bin or they are on the go. The organisers hope to eventually roll the scheme out nationwide.

The 'Waste-Water' Park in Germany

The region of North Rhine-Westphalia in the west of German has one water system which draws its resources from the river, canals, rainwater, and waste water. If the idea of getting your drinking water from waste water makes your stomach churn, you might think the residents of the west German state feel the same. But a water recycling park has been created, so residents can actually watch a duplicate water treatment system so they understand that it works and it's completely safe.

Recycling Mall in Sweden

ReTuna Återbruksgalleria, which can be translated as **"ReTuna Recycling Gallery"** is one of the malls in the south of Sweden which aims to purely and simply sell recycled, up-cycled, and sustainable goods to their customers.

Offering a variety of products to its customers such as furniture, repairable products, sports equipment, or clothing, the shopping center also donates unsold products to charities and so meets people's needs. Products to be recycled and sold are supplied by users leaving unused products in recycling warehouses located in certain locations.

Recycling Food Waste in the UK

In the United Kingdom, a company called **Biogen** aims to generate clean and renewable energy such as electricity, biogas, and biofertilizer from food waste. This company supplies food waste from households, supermarkets, restaurants, food manufacturers, or hotels into their 7-production facility. Biogen usually generates electricity and bio-fertilizer by transforming almost 250,000 tons of food waste.

Recycling Hygiene Products in Canada

Knowaste, a Canadian-based company founded in 1989, aims to produce different products by hygiene products for women, recycling diapers and absorbent hygiene products (AHP). Knowaste produces a solution to separate these waste products from plastic and fibers, then transform these separated parts into products such as composite building materials, pet waste, and cardboard industrial pipes.

Global and International Recycling Events

Global Recycling Day – 18 March annually
Global Recycling Day was created in 2018 to help recognise, and celebrate, the importance recycling plays in preserving our precious primary resources and securing the future of our planet. It is a day for the world to come together and put the planet first.
https://www.globalrecyclingday.com/

The international Recycling Week / 21-24 June 2021
Waste & Recycling Middle East and Africa magazine and Recycling Today Media Group present the international Recycling Week, a virtual event that aims to connect delegates to the latest information and technology developments in the fast changing recycling industry. The 4-day virtual event targets 4 main segments - Plastics, Paper, Metals and Construction and Demolition (C&D) Recycling. Each day dedicated to one of the sectors will witness keynote speeches, panel discussions, presentations, tech talks and more.
https://www.wasterecyclingmea.com/recycling-week

ISRI 2022 Convention & Expo / 21-24 March 2022
Las Vegas, USA
The recycling industry's largest in-person event. Be part of the fun, networking, education, and recycling community once again.
https://isri2022.org/

2022 BIR World Recycling Convention / October 16 -18, 2022
Dubai, United Arab Emirates
https://www.bir.org/

E-Waste World Conference & Expo / 30 November to 1 December 2022
The Frankfurt Messe, Germany
This physical two-day international five-stream conference and free-to-attend exhibition will showcase the latest recycling technologies, materials-recovery solutions, circular electronics innovations, sustainable materials, non-toxic substitutes, and end-of-life strategies for electronic waste, including electric vehicle batteries and photovoltaics, as well as the regulatory and business models to help reduce the environmental impact of all forms of consumer and industrial e-waste.
https://www.ewaste-expo.com/

Recycle Now - Recycle Now is a campaign to encourage people to recycle more things more often. From recycling more everyday items like glass and plastic bottles and unwanted electrical goods to reducing our food waste, re-using carrier bags or trying out new things like home composting, there's lots we can all do to help cut back on the amount of waste we send to landfill.

https://www.youtube.com/user/RecycleNowCampaign/videos

Institute of Scrap Recycling Industries - ISRI is the voice of the scrap recycling industry, an association of companies that process, broker, and consume scrap commodities.

https://www.youtube.com/user/ISRI1987/videos

Rockaway Recycling - Rockaway Recycling, Rockaway NJ, has been an industry leader for many years recycling scrap metal in the Tri-State area. By educating community on how to recycle, we have kept millions of pounds of material from being dumped in landfills.

https://www.youtube.com/user/RockawayRecycling/videos

ECO Green Equipment, USA | Tire Recycling Equipment and Shredders - ECO Green Equipment, USA, has been designing and manufacturing equipment for the recycling industry for over a decade and is emerging as a leader in providing cost effective turnkey tire recycling systems. Our focus is to provide custom designed tire recycling systems that deliver optimum production for a variety of applications such as TDF (Tire Derived Fuel), wire-free rubber mulch, crumb rubber.

https://www.youtube.com/user/EcoGreenEquipment/videos

Rumpke CleanAndGreen - Rumpke Waste & Recycling has been committed to keeping neighborhoods and businesses clean and green since 1932 by providing environmentally friendly waste disposal solutions and recycling options.

https://www.youtube.com/user/RumpkeCleanAndGreen/videos

Zero Waste Europe - Zero Waste Europe (ZWE) proposes to re-design our society in a way that all superfluous waste is eliminated and everything that is produced can be re-used, repaired, composted or recycled back into the system.

https://www.youtube.com/channel/UCqMnEtOQI168gv3iBLJtf3g/videos

Ryan Hickman - This is Ryan Hickman, President of Ryan's Recycling Company. Help me save the planet by recycling!

https://www.youtube.com/user/damionhickmandesign/videos

Recycle BC - Recycle BC is a non-profit organization responsible for residential packaging a printed paper recycling throughout British Columbia.

https://www.youtube.com/user/RecyclingInBC/videos

re3 recycling - Our YouTube films provide information, advice and support to help re3 area residents waste less and recycle more and better.

https://www.youtube.com/channel/UC3PltzrhUu0qukm7JF0SO9g/videos

Smalltime Recycling - This channel is focused on reusing, recycling and bringing awareness to the wastefulness of America.

https://www.youtube.com/user/chuferd/videos

Trash is for Tossers - Trash Is For Tossers is a #ZeroWaste editorial platform that shows living a low or zero waste lifestyle can be easy, cost-effective, accessible, and fun! Here you'll find Zero Waste tips, DIY recipes, and sustainability tricks in order to live a waste-free or low-waste life.

https://www.youtube.com/channel/UCgjw6tZNyjR_8zIFDsIPpww

Rob Greenfield - This channel is a source to educate, inspire and help others to live more sustainable, equitable and just lives. Videos frequently cover sustainable & simple living, growing your own food, minimalism, off the grid living, zero waste, tiny houses and permaculture.

https://www.youtube.com/channel/UCKirXBZV7hE4Fws3VSdYkRQ

ARA Recycling - Altstoff Recycling Austria AG is the market leader in Austria in the field of packaging collection and recycling systems and undertakes to take back their recycling and recycling obligations in accordance with the Packaging Ordinance. The ARA is owned by domestic companies and acts as a non-profit company not profit-oriented.

https://www.youtube.com/user/arasocial/videos

The Recycling Partnership - We believe that recycling is fundamental to a healthy environment and economy. Every day, we work hand-in-hand with communities and companies, continuously innovating to improve recycling systems.

https://www.youtube.com/channel/UCsszdB7PiQ3Ck2z33zBCh3A/videos

Mattress Recycling Council - The Mattress Recycling Council (MRC) is a non-profit organization that develops and operates mattress recycling programs in Connecticut, California and Rhode Island beginning in 2016.

https://www.youtube.com/user/mattressrecycling/videos

The Top 10 Recycling Stars

Recycling International Magazine has made a list of the top 10 in the global recycling arena to celebrate the inspiring and determined entrepreneurs, companies and projects that have made our industry what it is today.

#1 Jean-Philippe Fusier, owner and CEO of MTB Recycling (France)

Fusier is mostly known as a recycling machinery producer operating under the same MTB brand name. But, as with most equipment suppliers, MTB began as a scrap recycler and today manufacture and scrap recycling still go hand in hand. Based in Trept, west of Lyon, Fusier and his dedicated team process some 50 000 tons of non-ferrous per year, mainly copper and aluminum cable.

We see Fusier as a visionary and innovative recycler, rather than motivated by making ever more money. What drives him is helping to create a healthy environment for future generations and to secure the future of his company. In recent economic rough years and challenging scrap market conditions, Fusier had the guts to invest EUR 17 million in a new facility to ramp up production and shredding capacity.

The eco-design plant delivers 80% of the required electrical supply thanks to solar panels and a series of batteries. MTB also has a fleet of electric vehicles along with a sports hall, canteen and greenhouses for employees to enjoy some gardening during their lunch hour.

Fusier is patron of the SeaCleaners association, founded in 2016 by French ecological adventurer Yves Bourgnon to eliminate ocean plastic pollution. MTB is a technical partner of the foundation's Manta project. The sailing ship Manta can be best described as a floating plastics recycling facility and research lab. The vessel is due to be deployed in the coastal waters of the Mediterranean in 2022-23.

#2 Johanna Leshabane, founder of Bophelo Recycling (South Africa)

The South African entrepreneur describes Bophelo Recycling as a 'waste buy-back centre' that collects recyclable PET plastic from informal settlements, households and schools in the Ermelo region. Leshabane built her business from the ground up and now has 11 full-time staff and 20 part-time waste pickers. The company has collected over 45 tons of plastic scrap since it launched in 2017 and the founder cites a 79% increase in collection volumes since it opened its doors. She says the power of a grassroots enterprise like hers, employing local people and teaching them practical skills, is vital in developing nations across Africa. 'I hope to expand operations to other towns and rural settlements in the coming months. I want to teach more people how they can start their own recycling business.'

#3 Craig Thompson, CEO of Areera Intelligent Screen Recycling (UK)

At an early stage, this e-scrap plastics recycling expert saw that China's scrap import restriction would have a huge impact on recycling businesses across Europe and North America. 'We need to press the reset button as end markets for e-scrap plastics are changing forever,' he warned in an interview with RI in 2018.

Thompson has been active in electronics recycling since 1999. He launched the UK's first franchised e-scrap collection system in 2005 and opened one of the country's largest electronics recycling facilities. Over the past ten years, Thompson has worked with the majority of e-scrap recyclers in Europe, Canada and the USA on outlets for their e-scrap plastics.

Before the pandemic, Thompson was a global citizen, constantly on the move and his business card had mobile numbers for Hong Kong, UK, Netherlands, Brazil, Latvia and North America. For his latest project he settled down in the English region he grew up, Yorkshire, where he has set up and leads Areera, claimed to be the UK's most advanced automated robotic recycling facility for flat panel displays, notebooks and x-ray separation of electronics and e-scrap plastics.

#4 Surendra Borad Patawari, founder and ceo of Gemini Corporation (Belgium/India)

'Recycling is my passion, recycling is my life,' said Borad Patawari in January 2020 at the International Electronics Recycling Congress after having received the congress' honorary award in recognition of his lifetime's work in the sourcing, processing and reuse of raw materials.

Patawari founded Gemini in 1989 and the company has grown into an international sourcing and supply organization with operations spanning more than 40 countries. The product portfolio at Gemini includes core divisions of plastics, steel, rubber and paper.

Besides being a successful businessman, Patawari is also known for his commitment to creating a social impact through multiple long-term initiatives in India. He has adopted 11 Indian villages to support their medical needs; built and operates two schools for 400 students; and supports the planting and maintenance of more than 100 000 trees. Patawari is also a respected contributor to the market updates in this magazine.

#5 Purified Metal Company (The Netherlands)

Launched in 2019 as the world's first site for safely recycling contaminated steel, the EUR 70 million PMC facility in the north of the Netherlands processes steel scrap containing asbestos and chromium-6 as well as organic contamination from large demolition objects such as chemical installations, drilling platforms and trains. The end product is a clean, premium raw material for steel mills, branded Purified Metal Blocks.

A former Soviet submarine that was dismantled and scrapped at the Janssen Recycling yard in the Port of Rotterdam had the honor of being the first major demolition project in which contaminated scrap was processed at PMC. The company plans to set up similar facilities at other locations around the world.

#6 Adam Minter, author of Junkyard Planet (USA)

Minter comes from a Minnesota scrapyard family and has made it his life's work to document the ins and outs of the global recycling industry. Having lived in Singapore for years, he is very familiar with developments in the Asian market. He has also covered the African scrap market extensively – see the cover story in Recycling International from October 2015 – telling the story of pioneers in Ghana. Minter writes articles and columns for Bloomberg and travelled the world for his best-seller 'Junkyard Planet'. The book was followed by another popular title 'Second Hand'. A third book is currently in the works.

#7 TES (USA)

TES uses proprietary in-house technology to recover nickel, lithium and cobalt from car batteries. The company currently has 45 recycling plants in more than 20 countries and is active in China. In March, it opened a new battery recycling facility in Singapore which relies on a hydro-metallurgical process. The site can handle 14 tons of lithium-ion batteries, the equivalent of 280 000 smart phones, every day. TES manages a 90% recovery rate and extracts battery materials with 99% purity.

#8 Doug Kramer, owner of Kramer Metals/Spectrum Alloys (USA)

As with so many fellow recyclers, Kramer Metals of Vernon, Los Angeles was challenged by Covid-19. Recycling International talked with Kramer in the first weeks of the pandemic. 'The world has shut down,' the former ISRI chair lamented. 'There's no open or free movement of scrap and that is scary.' At the same time, he was optimistic about the future. 'Although the uncertainty of how long this will take hurts, I believe we will be OK and our business will survive this crisis.'

Kramer Metals has proved to be resilient. The company, as with the entire scrap recycling industry across the US and worldwide, was considered part of an essential sector.

#9 Dhawal Shah, managing director of Metco Marketing (India)

Besides being a scrap trader running a profitable business, Shah is a true ambassador for his country and its recycling sector. During the latest BIR convention, Shah expressed deep sorrow at the Covid pandemic's devastating recent impact on India: 'It's beyond imagination; we paid a heavy toll,' he said.

Talking with this commerce graduate from Mumbai, helps to better understand India. 'We are not there yet, we have to undo decades of inefficiency and corruption. But the good days will come. This is all work in progress,' he told RI in 2018. The good news is, India has already the world's sixth-largest economy with 65% of its population under the age of 35. Every day, 40 km of new road is being added and the country already has more than a billion telephone connections.

Shah is vice-president of the Metal Recycling Association of India and serves on the metals committee of the Federation of Indian Chambers of Commerce and Industry. In June 2021 Shah was appointed the new divisional president for non-ferrous at BIR.

#10 Murat Bayram, director non-ferrous at EMR (Germany/UK)

'You need to be an all-rounder to survive in scrap metal trading,' says Bayram. Certainly, this scrap trader from Hamburg fits the bill. One can hardly imagine a congress or online event without him in the line-up. Bayram frequently climbs on to conference stages to share his views on the industry's ups-and-downs. He always advocates the interest of the recycling sector in general rather than promoting the company he represents.

It's Bayram's style of presentation people enjoy: open, enthusiastic and with humor. His comment are always illustrated with personal, close-to-home experiences. Example: in a recent online BIR panel discussing electronics design for recycling and repair, Bayram explained how his sons' car toy remote control failed but could not be fixed due to the device's complex contents. The recycling industry could use more storytellers such as Murat Bayram!

References

Recycling Basics, United States Environmental Protection Agency (EPA), in
https://www.epa.gov/recycle/recycling-basics

Recycling Terms & Definitions, in https://www.terracycle.com/en-US/pages/definitions

What is Recycling and why is Recycling Important, in https://www.conserve-energy-future.com/why-is-recycling-important.php

Brad Smith, What are the 3 types of Recycling?, 2020. In
https://www.vanellagroupmn.com/what-are-the-3-types-of-recycling

From a linear to a circular economy, Government of the Netherlands, in
https://www.government.nl/topics/circular-economy/from-a-linear-to-a-circular-economy

Recycling and the circular economy: what's the difference?, in
https://ellenmacarthurfoundation.org/articles/recycling-and-the-circular-economy-whats-the-difference

Recycling and the circular economy, Zero Waste Scotland, in
https://www.zerowastescotland.org.uk/circular-economy/recycling

This are the 15 world's biggest recycling companies, Waste Management World, in
https://waste-management-world.com/a/this-are-the-15-worlds-biggest-recycling-companies

List of Recycling and Waste Management Publications, Harmony Enterprises, Inc. in
https://harmony1.com/recycling-and-waste-management-publications/

Recycling: the countries which are best and worst, in
https://www.lovemoney.com/gallerylist/89902/recycling-countries-best-worst

6 Creative Recycling Efforts From Around the Globe, Mental Floss, 2017, in
https://www.mentalfloss.com/article/94632/6-creative-recycling-efforts-around-globe

6 bright ideas in 2021 that are helping end plastic waste, Alliance to End Plastic Waste,
https://endplasticwaste.org/our-stories/6-bright-ideas-in-2021

Top 6 Recycling and Reuse Initiatives from Around the Globe, INHABITAT, in
https://inhabitat.com/top-6-recycling-and-reuse-initiatives-from-around-the-globe/

Top 8 Innovative Recycling Apps That Make A Difference, Apiumhub, in
https://apiumhub.com/tech-blog-barcelona/innovative-recycling-apps/

Used into green: Top 5 recycling innovations, in https://www.dw.com/en/used-into-green-top-5-recycling-innovations/a-42202769

10 Nonprofits Reusing and Recycling to Help Kids, 2017, in https://www.budgetdumpster.com/blog/10-recycling-nonprofits-helping-kids/

The Coolest Non Profit Recycling Programs You've Never Heard Of, in https://www.organicauthority.com/live-grow/the-coolest-non-profit-recycling-programs-youve-never-heard-of

Recycling for Charity - Programs that Reduce Waste & Give Back, Matt Bradbury, 2016, in https://www.buschsystems.com/resource-center/page/recycling-for-charity-programs-that-reduce-waste-give-back

The Best Recycling Initiatives Around the Globe, https://www.recyclingbins.co.uk/blog/the-best-recycling-initiatives-around-the-globe/

6 Recycling Projects around the World, in https://www.ecodaption.com/6-recycling-projects-around-the-world/

Dr. Abdul-Sattar Nizami, Recycling Prospects in Saudi Arabia, 2020. In https://www.ecomena.org/recycling-in-saudi-arabia/

Businesses that Recycle in Saudi Arabia and Turn Trash Into Cash, Aabiya Noman Baqai, DESTINATION, 2015. In https://destinationksa.com/recycling-business-saudi-arabia-turning-trash-cash/

The top 10 of our Top 100, Recycling International, 2021. In https://recyclinginternational.com/business/top-10-in-our-top-100/45541/

45 Recycling YouTube Channels, Feed spot, https://blog.feedspot.com/recycling_youtube_channels/